DATE DUE

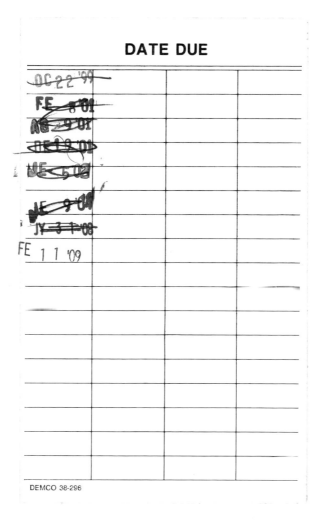

OC 22 '99		
FE 8 01		
AG 9 01		
DE 18 01		
JE 5 02		
JE 9 04		
JY 31 08		
FE 11 '09		

The Law of Obscenity and Pornography

by
Margaret C. Jasper

Oceana's Legal Almanac Series:
Law for the Layperson

1996
Oceana Publications, Inc.
Dobbs Ferry, N.Y.

Jasper, Margaret C. The Law of Obscenity and Pornography

ISBN: 0-379-11231-0

Copyright 1996 by Oceana Publications, Inc.

Manufactured in the United States of America on acid-free paper.

Legal Almanac Series
ISSN: 1075-7376

ABOUT THE AUTHOR

MARGARET C. JASPER is an attorney engaged in the general practice of law in South Salem, New York, concentrating in the areas of personal injury and entertainment law. Ms. Jasper holds a Juris Doctor degree from Pace University School of Law, White Plains, New York, is a member of the New York and Connecticut bars, and is certified to practice before the United States District Courts for the Southern and Eastern Districts of New York. She has been appointed to the panel of arbitrators of the American Arbitration Association and the law guardian panel for the Family Court of the State of New York, and is a New York State licensed real estate broker and member of the Westchester County Board of Realtors, operating as Jasper Real Estate, in South Salem, New York.

Ms. Jasper is the author of the following legal almanacs: Juvenile Justice and Children's Law; Marriage and Divorce; Estate Planning; The Law of Contracts; The Law of Dispute Resolution; Law for the Small Business Owner; The Law of Personal Injury; Real Estate Law for the Homeowner and Broker; Everyday Legal Forms; Dictionary of Selected Legal Terms; The Law of Medical Malpractice; The Law of Product Liability; The Law of No-Fault Insurance; The Law of Immigration; The Law of Libel and Slander; The Law of Buying and Selling; Elder Law; The Right to Die; and AIDS Law.

To My Husband Chris

Your love and support
are my motivation and inspiration

TABLE OF CONTENTS

APPENDICIES

INTRODUCTION

"I know it when I see it." Referring to obscenity, these famous words were spoken by U.S. Supreme Court Justice Potter Stewart in *Jacobellis v. Ohio (1964)*. If only it were as easy as Justice Potter stated, the courts would not be continually called upon to intervene and make such determinations.

The law of obscenity has evolved considerably since the first cases appeared in the courts. In part, this is due to the "new morality" of the 1970's. Prior to that time, there were strict controls on the print and broadcast media. Children of the 1950's were rarely exposed to anything remotely "indecent." For example, the parents on popular sitcoms slept in twin beds (e.g. *I Love Lucy* and *The Dick Van Dyke Show*).

This legal almanac explores the law of obscenity and pornography. It sets forth the evolution of the relevant case law, including constitutional considerations. Related issues, such as child pornography, and the relationship between pornography and violence are explored.

Finally, the almanac discusses the status of the current law, including the most recent legislation affecting materials available through the internet and various on-line services.

The Appendix provides tables of applicable statutes, and other pertinent information and data. The Glossary contains definitions of many of the terms used throughout the almanac.

CHAPTER 1:

OBSCENITY AND THE FIRST AMENDMENT

In General

Throughout history, courts have struggled to define pornography and obscenity. The term "pornography" has generally been used to describe sexually explicit material. The term "obscenity" refers to the legal definition of whether such materials are protected under the First Amendment guarantees of free speech and free press. Material which is deemed obscene is not constitutionally protected.

The burden of determining whether something is obscene, however, has been placed ultimately on the United States Supreme Court. The Court has attempted to formulate certain tests to make this determination, usually basing their decision on contemporary moral standards. However, a major problem exists in that what one person may deem "pornographic," another may perceive as "artistic expression."

The First Amendment

The First Amendment to the United States Constitution provides that:

> Congress shall make no law respecting an establishment of religion, or prohibiting the free exercise thereof; *or abridging the freedom of speech, or of the press*, or the right of the people peaceably to assemble, and to petition the Government for a redress of grievances.

The First Amendment has been cited as the "protector" of free speech forbidding, among other things, governmental censorship. Not all speech, however, is protected. The First Amendment does not protect, for example, libelous statements about another individual.

It is unlikely that the materials currently deemed permissible would have ever been afforded constitutional protection in 1791 when the amendment was ratified.   In fact, it is more likely that the publishers would be jailed.

Modern-day judicial decisions on a number of constitutional issues simply would not have been contemplated by the original drafters. However, it has been held that the constitution is subject to interpretation as it relates to the times.

The American Civil Liberties Union (ACLU)

The American Civil Liberties Union (ACLU) is a strong proponent of First Amendment rights.   Ironically, despite the ACLU's condemnation of child exploitation, their advocacy of the First Amendment has placed them on the side of the child pornography industry on a number of occasions.

The ACLU believes that control of the child pornography industry should not be fought on First Amendment grounds, but that stricter statutory controls governing child sexual abuse should be the preferred method.

In this way, the actual offenders, i.e., the producers of child pornography, would be prosecuted for engaging in illegal behavior. The ACLU believes that the publishers and distributors of the material should not be held accountable as they are protected under the First Amendment.

Of course, the ACLU has many critics who denounce their reasoning, maintaining that the First Amendment does not protect all printed material, and in no event should it ever protect child pornographers.

The topic of child pornography is further discussed in Chapter 5.

CHAPTER 2:

LEGISLATION AND CASE LAW

Early Legislative History

In this country, significant state and federal government intervention in the area of censorship of obscene materials did not occur until the mid to late 1800's. Prior to that time, there were some state laws criminalizing obscenity, but only sporadic convictions were obtained.

By the end of the nineteenth century, however, the majority of states had some type of law prohibiting obscenity. In addition, the federal government had enacted a number of such laws, the earliest being the Anti-Obscenity Act of 1873 which banned the mailing of any "obscene, lewd, lascivious, or filthy ... publication" (U.S.C., Title 18, §1461).

The *Hicklin* Test

Through the early twentieth century, American courts applied the standard of obscenity articulated by an English court in the 1868 decision in *Regina v. Hicklin*, known as the *Hicklin* test.

The *Hicklin* court apparently made its decision based on the content of isolated passages of the book rather than as a whole. Further, the Court asked whether the "tendency of the matter ... is to deprave and corrupt those whose minds are open to such immoral influences, and into whose hands a publication of this sort may fall."

These two issues: (1) isolated passages; and (2) the susceptible person, were paramount in the court's decision making, and formed the basis for the two-part *Hicklin* test.

U.S. v. One Book Called Ulysses - Rejecting *Hicklin*

In 1933, the *Hicklin* Test met its final demise in *U.S. v. One Book Called Ulysses*, 5 F. Supp. 182 (1933), wherein the U.S. District Court rejected the "isolated passages" and the "susceptible person" doctrines.

In his opinion, Judge John Woolsey held that the preferred test should be based on the dominant effect the "entire book" would have on an "average person."

Roth v. U.S. - Setting a New Standard

In *Roth v. U.S.*, 354 U.S. 476 (1957), the U.S. Supreme Court upheld the constitutionality of the federal Anti-Obscenity Act of 1873, and the conviction of Mr. Samuel Roth, a New York publisher and seller of books and magazines.

The *Hicklin* test met its final demise when the court rejected the test as being unconstitutionally restrictive of the freedoms of speech and the press, and replaced it with a new standard similar to that enunciated by Judge Woolsey in *Ulysses*.

The new obscenity test would focus on "whether to the *average person*, applying contemporary community standards, the dominant theme of the material *taken as a whole* appeals to the prurient interest."

The Court further ruled that although ideas having even the slightest redeeming social importance are protected, obscenity is not constitutionally protected under the First and Fourteenth Amendments because it "utterly lacks any redeeming social importance."

Jacobellis v. State of Ohio - The Value Test

In *Jacobellis v. State of Ohio*, 378 U.S. 184 (1964), the U.S. Supreme Court reversed the conviction of Mr. Jacobellis, an Ohio theater manager. Mr. Jacobellis had been convicted of violating a state statute which prohibited the showing of obscene films.

The majority opinion expanded on the *Roth* test by holding that materials which have literary, scientific or artistic value, or are of social importance, or advocate ideas, are constitutionally protected even if they involve sexual matter.

Further, the Court stated that to be obscene, the material must be "utterly without redeeming social importance." Although Justice Brennan had used this language in the *Roth* decision, it was not made a part of the obscenity test until *Jacobellis*.

Memoirs v. Massachusetts - Refining *Roth*

In *Memoirs v. Massachusetts*, 383 U.S. 413 (1966), The United States Supreme Court refined the test of obscenity and set forth three elements which must be established:

1. The dominant theme of the material taken as a whole appeals to prurient interest in sex;

2. The material is patently offensive because it affronts contemporary community standards relating to the description or representation of sexual matters; and

3. The material is utterly without redeeming social value.

Ginsberg v. State of New York - Sale to Minors

In *Ginsberg v. State of New York*, 390 U.S. 629 (1968), the U.S. Supreme Court affirmed the conviction of Samuel Ginsberg for violation of a New York statute which prohibited the sale of obscene material to minors under the age of 17.

The Court deferred to the state legislature's determination that exposure to such material was harmful to minors, and found this to be a rational reason for enacting the statute.

Stanley v. Georgia - Privacy of the Home

In *Stanley v. Georgia* 394 U.S. 557 (1969), the U.S. Supreme Court reversed the conviction of Mr. Stanley, and struck down a Georgia statute which made it illegal for a person to possess obscene matter, even in the privacy of one's own home.

Miller v. California - A Landmark Decision

In 1973, the United States Supreme Court made sweeping changes in the obscenity test, and abandoned the requirement that the material be "utterly without redeeming social value."

As set forth in the majority decision in *Miller v. California*, 413 U.S. 15 (1973), the Court held that the test of obscenity would be determined by the following three-part test:

> 1. Prurient Interest - Whether the average person, applying contemporary community standards, would find that the work, taken as a whole, appeals to the prurient interest;
>
> 2. Patently Offensive - Whether the work depicts or describes, in a patently offensive way, sexual conduct specifically defined by the applicable state law; and
>
> 3. Value - Whether the work, taken as a whole, lacks serious literary, artistic, political or scientific value.

If the work (1) appeals to the prurient interest; and (2) is patently offensive, then in order to be constitutionally protected, the Court held that it must meet the third prong, i.e., it must contain serious literary, artistic, political or scientific value.

The Court set forth some permissible examples of prohibited behavior to guide states in formulating their obscenity statutes, as follows:

1. Patently offensive representations or descriptions of ultimate sexual acts, normal or perverted, actual or simulated.

2. Patently offensive representations or descriptions of masturbation, excretory functions, and lewd exhibition of the genitals.

Community Standards and The Reasonable Person

The first two prongs of the *Miller* test concern issues of fact which are generally decided by a jury applying "contemporary community standards" as its measuring stick. However, the definition of "community" is much broader than one's "neighborhood." For example, in New York, the "community" has been held to refer to the entire State of New York

In *Pope v. Illinois*, 481 U.S. 497 (1987), the U.S. Supreme Court evaluated this standard as it applied to the third prong of the test. The Court redefined the part of the test concerning the literary, artistic, political or scientific value of the material, holding that the standard would now be measured by whether "a reasonable person" would find such value in the material, taken as a whole.

CHAPTER 3:

THE ATTORNEY GENERAL'S
COMMISSION ON PORNOGRAPHY

In 1986, the Attorney General's Commission on Pornography, formed by Attorney General Edwin Meese, issued a comprehensive report on the effect of pornographic materials on society.

Perhaps the Commission's most significant finding was that there was a link between sexually violent materials and antisocial — and sometimes illegal — acts of sexual violence. The report discusses the numerous adverse effects which, according to those who testified before the Commission, are in some way attributed to their involvement with pornography.

The report also sets forth 92 recommendations for federal, state and local governments to combat the problem. However, the report was met with strong opposition by the American Civil Liberties Union, which stated that its recommendations, if put into action, would be unconstitutional.

Selected excerpts from the Final Report by the Attorney General's Commission on Pornography are set forth in the Appendix.

CHAPTER 4:

CENSORSHIP

In General

Although pornography clearly has its opponents, the issue of censorship raises concerns by many about restrictions on the constitutional guarantees of free speech and a free press. This is the primary concern of the American Civil Liberties Union (ACLU), one of the nation's largest First Amendment watchdog organizations. Several of the most significant censorship rulings are set forth below.

Censorship and The United States Post Office

In 1942, the U.S. Post Office began denying second-class special mailing privileges to publications it deemed immoral or which did not contribute to the public good. Of course, this resulted in a large increase in mailing costs for the publishers.

After its second class mailing permit was revoked, *Esquire* Magazine challenged this Post Office regulation in the U.S. District Court, where it lost. The ruling was appealed to the U.S. Court of Appeals for the D.C. Circuit, which reversed the lower court ruling.

The case was then appealed to the U.S. Supreme Court, which affirmed the Court of Appeals decision, holding that restrictions on second class mail rates cannot be based on a Post Office determination that certain publications do not "contribute to the public good."

Censorship and the Motion Picture Industry

In the early 1900's, the U.S. Supreme Court held that the First Amendment did not apply to the motion picture industry because it was a business. This ruling led to intense censorship of motion pictures.

The Supreme Court changed its position in 1952 under its ruling in the case of *Burstyn v. Wilson*, 343 U.S. 495 (1952). The *Burstyn* case involved a movie entitled *The Miracle*, which was met with intense criticism by religious groups. The film was subsequently banned by the New York courts.

On appeal, the Supreme Court held that the First and Fourteenth Amendment protections were not forfeited simply because a movie is made for profit, although the obscenity test remained applicable. Underlying the Court's change in position was its reasoning that motion pictures, like literary materials, were an important medium for the communication of political and social ideas.

Censorship and the Theater

The most significant decision concerning censorship and the theater involves the rock musical *Hair*. The road company was barred from performing in a city-leased theater in Chattanooga, Tennessee because the directors of the theater board (the "board") deemed the production obscene.

The promoter of the production, Southeastern Promotions, Ltd., filed suit (*Southeastern Promotions, Ltd. v. Steve Conrad, 95 S. Ct. 1239 (1975)*). *Following a hearing before the U.S. District Court, the jury: (1) concurred that the production was obscene; and (2) found that the group nudity and simulated sex acts were not speech, and thus not protected under the First Amendment.*

In 1975, the U.S. Supreme Court, on appeal, reversed the District Court's ruling without making a determination on whether or not the production was obscene. Instead, the Court found that the board's action in denying use of the theater constituted a system of *prior restraint* that violated the First Amendment.

The Court concluded that the burden of proving that the material was unprotected rested on the censor, i.e., the board, and the board was responsible for initiating the judicial proceedings. The Court also pointed out that "any restraint prior to judicial review can be imposed only for a specified brief period .. for the purpose of preserving the status quo," and that "prompt judicial determination must be assured."

FCC Censorship of the Broadcast Media

Broadcasting is regulated by the Federal Communications Commission (FCC), an independent regulatory agency under the federal government. The FCC is empowered to oversee the licensing of broadcasters. Those who violate FCC regulations may incur substantial fines, or have their license revoked.

However, the Federal Communications Act of 1934 specifically prohibits the FCC from censoring broadcasters, and from interfering with their right of free speech. In enforcing its obscenity standards, the FCC has been met with numerous First Amendment challenges.

The FCC has remained uninvolved in the regulation of cable television programming. Because cable television does not use the airwaves, the FCC has declined to claim jurisdiction over this entity.

Censorship in the Computer Age

Two federal courts recently struck down The Communications Decency Act of 1996, signed into law on February 8, 1996 by President Clinton. This Act bans the transmission of obscene materials to minors via broadcast media, including the internet and various on-line services. The case is presently on appeal to the United States Supreme Court which is likely to rule on this issue in the near future.

Further discussion of obscenity and the Internet is set forth in Chapter 7.

CHAPTER 5:

CHILD PORNOGRAPHY

In General

It is a very disturbing fact that child pornography and prostitution are highly organized, multi-million dollar industries that operate in our society on a nationwide scale. In 1977, Congressional hearings were held on the subject of child pornography, also known as "kiddie porn."

Witnesses who appeared before Congress told nightmare tales about small children who were kidnapped by pornographers, or sold to pornographers by their parents. Outraged federal and state legislators have since attempted to enact laws to combat this widespread problem. Following the 1977 Congressional hearings, two federal statutes were passed, as discussed below.

The Protection of Children from Sexual Exploitation Act of 1977

Shortly after the close of the 1977 Congressional hearings on child pornography, Congress passed the Protection of Children from Sexual Exploitation Act of 1977 (The 1977 Act). The 1977 Act prohibits the production of any sexually explicit material using a child under the age of sixteen, if such material is destined for, or has already traveled in interstate commerce.

In dealing with already produced material, Congress concerned itself with the commercial aspect of the industry, and prohibited the transportation, shipping , mailing or receipt of child pornography in interstate commerce for the purpose of sale or distribution for sale.

Violations of the Act carry penalties of 10 years in prison and/or a $10,000 fine. In response to allegations that children were being sold by their parents into the pornography industry, the law was made applicable to parents or other custodians who knowingly permit a child to participate in the production of sexually explicit material.

Sexually explicit material under the 1977 Act is defined as any conduct involving sexual intercourse, bestiality, masturbation, sado-masochistic abuse, or lewd exhibition of the genitals or pubic area.

Unfortunately, the statute was not particularly effective. By its own language, the statute failed to prohibit the exchange of child pornography if it was done without compensation. As a result, the child pornography industry simply went underground with its activities. In addition, Congress was constrained to add a provision that the prohibited material also meet the *Miller* test of obscenity in order to satisfy constitutional challenges.

The Child Protection Act of 1984

Because the 1977 Act proved to be of little practical value, Congress attempted to strengthen its provisions by enacting new legislation. In 1984, President Reagan signed into law the Child Protection Act (The 1984 Act).

The 1984 Act gave prosecutors a much stronger weapon in their fight against the use of children in pornographic materials. It eliminated the requirement that child pornography distribution be undertaken for the purpose of "sale." It also did away with the *Miller* obscenity test, and the age of protection was raised to eighteen. In addition, penalties under the 1984 Act were greatly increased over those set forth in the 1977 Act, and a provision for criminal and civil forfeiture was included.

State Legislation

In their "parens patrie" role as guardians of abused and/or neglected children, the state has the primary interest in protecting its children. Virtually all states prohibit the production and distribution of child pornography. The criminal statutory scheme concerning obscenity and child pornography contained in New York State's Penal Code is discussed in Chapter 8.

A table of state child pornography statutes is set forth in the Appendix.

The Nature of the Child Pornography Industry

The structure of the child pornography industry ranges from individual abusers who are out to satisfy their own perverted desires to highly organized, profit-seeking operations, many of which are suspected to have a connection with organized crime.

Profile of the Child Pornographer

According to the Attorney General's Commission on Pornography, child pornographers come from a broad range of religious, ethnic and socioeconomic backgrounds and occupations. Offenders often exhibit low self-esteem and difficulty relating intimately with others

The Commission has defined child pornographers as either "situational" or "preferential" molesters.

A situational molester is one who acts out of some serious sexual or psychological need, but who chooses children as victims only when they are readily and safely accessible.

The preferential molester, also known as a *pedophile* exhibits a clear sexual preference for children, and their deviant desires can only be satisfied by children.

These behaviors have been noted by experts to be an addiction which, like other addictive behaviors, can be controlled but not cured.

Profile of the Child Victim

The child victims also come from a wide variety of family backgrounds, including all socioeconomic classes and religions. They range in age from infancy through adolescence.

Young children are often victimized by someone they know, e.g. a neighbor or family member. Many crave adult affection, and are lured into the behavior in an effort to obtain approval by adult authority figures. Others are kidnapped by strangers and forced into submission.

Adolescent victims are often runaways or teens engaged in criminal behavior, such as prostitution. Their economic situation is usually precarious, and many are homeless. The pornographers prey on their vulnerability, often luring them with money and a place to stay.

The long-term effects on children who have been victims of child pornographers are devastating. They are generally unable to form normal sexual relationships with persons of the opposite sex. Many child victims fall into destructive lifestyles, such as drug and alcohol addiction, and many succumb to suicide.

The Cycle of Child Pornography

Following are common steps reportedly taken by child pornography publishers in introducing a child to pornographic activity:

1. Pornographic materials are shown to the child victim, e.g., for sex education purposes.

2. An attempt is made to convince the child victim that sex is acceptable and desirable.

3. Showing of child pornography is used to convince the child victim that other children are sexually active.

4. The showing of child pornography to the child victim desensitizes the child and lowers the child's inhibitions.

5. Sexual activity may occur during sessions.

6. Photographs or movies are taken of the sexual activity.

CHAPTER 6:

THE PORNOGRAPHY INDUSTRY

The business of the pornography industry generally includes the production and distribution of magazines, videocassettes, and films; computer sex services; peep shows; and telephone services, generally referred to as "dial-a-porn."

There is really no incentive to stop producing and distributing pornography. Everyone in the distribution chain is making money in this multi-billion dollar industry, including the telephone company, which has expanded its operations in order to handle the volume of "dial-a-porn" calls.

Pornography is big business. The profit margin for the producers and distributors of pornography is enormous. Law enforcement officials contend that the industry is controlled by organized crime due to its lucrative nature.

Due in large part to changing moral standards over the last twenty-five years, the audience has broadened. Pornographic materials are readily available. No longer does an individual have to travel to a dangerous, seedy part of town to avail him or herself of x-rated films, magazines, and other pornographic materials. Cable television, satellite television, video rentals, computers and telephone services bring a vast array of x-rated materials to the consumer in the privacy of his or her home.

Opponents of pornography contend that a number of other crimes are directly and indirectly related to the industry, including murder, rape, physical violence, prostitution, sexual abuse, and drugs. Further, the profits reaped from the industry are often used to support other criminal activities.

Based on testimony provided before it, the Attorney General's Commission on Pornography concluded that there was a direct link between pornography and the above crimes, as well as a number of other harmful, if not illegal, consequences.

Selected excerpts from the Final Report of the Attorney General's Commission on Pornography are set forth in the Appendix.

Anti-pornography activists have attempted to halt some of the operations, particularly those operating in the public, such as adult bookstores and peep shows.   By staging pickets of the establishments, they have had some success. However, the bottom line is that as long as there are consumers willing to support the pornography industry, it will thrive and prosper.

CHAPTER 7:

COMPUTERS AND THE INTERNET

In General

Regulating indecent material on the Internet and various other on-line services has become a challenging task. There is much concern over how to prevent a child from accessing sexual explicit materials and participating in sexually-related discussions through their computers, and still protect the First Amendment rights of adults to engage in constitutionally protected indecent speech. Congress has attempted to address this problem by passing legislation, which is further discussed below.

Many staunch First Amendment supporters contend that there should be no restrictions on adult access, and state that there is no need for federal laws regulating information which may be broadcast in "cyberspace." Opponents of restrictions argue that offensive images do not merely project themselves onto the screen, but that they must be sought out by the subscriber.

They believe that the burden of restricting child access should be placed upon parents and legal guardians who can use existing technology to prevent their children from accessing Internet sites which exhibit sexually explicit material. In practice, however, this is difficult, particularly since many children in this technological society are far more computer literate than their parents.

The Communications Decency Act of 1996

On February 8, 1996, President Clinton signed into law the Telecommunications Act of 1996 (the "Act"). Incorporated into the Act as Title V is the Communications Decency Act of 1996 (the "CDA"). The CDA was passed overwhelmingly by Congress.

The CDA generally bans the transmission of obscene materials to minors via broadcast media, including the Internet, making it a crime with a maximum of 2 years in prison and $250,000 in fines.

Critics of the CDA, most notably the ACLU, have argued that the legislation constitutes government censorship and the establishment of new speech crimes for the Internet and online communications. They argue that it fails to use the constitutionally required "least restrictive means" in regulating protected speech to obtain its goal, and invades the privacy rights of persons communicating online.

The text of the Communications Decency Act of 1996 is set forth in the Appendix.

ACLU v. Reno

On June 12, 1996, in *ACLU v. Reno*, the United States District Court for the Eastern District of Pennsylvania ruled that the CDA is unconstitutional on its face. The court held that portions of the CDA were too vague as well as too broad. The Justice Department filed an appeal of this ruling.

The Second Circuit Court of Appeals

On July 29, 1996, the Second Circuit Court of Appeals in New York similarly found that the CDA was overly broad because, in its efforts to protect children, it bans constitutionally protected indecent speech between adults. This challenged was brought by *The American Reporter*, an on-line newspaper. The court suggested that the burden to restrict access by children should be placed on their parents.

United States Supreme Court

In drafting the CDA, lawmakers expected there to be immediate constitutional challenges. Therefore, they included provisions in the law expediting review by the U.S. Supreme Court. Special panels of federal judges hear the cases first and the decision of the panel can be appealed directly to the Supreme Court.

It is expected that the court will announce its acceptance of either one or both of the above cases for review as early as September 1996.

CHAPTER 8:

THE NEW YORK PENAL CODE

In General

An examination of the crime of obscenity under the New York Penal Code is set forth in this section as a representative state statutory scheme which complies with the constitutional requirements of the First Amendment.

The Crime of Obscenity

Obscenity is defined in §235.00 of the New York Penal Code as follows:

1. Obscene - Any material or performance is "obscene" if:

   (a) the average person, applying contemporary community standards, would find that considered as a whole, its predominant appeal is to the prurient interest in sex; and

   (b) it depicts or describes in a patently offensive manner, actual or simulated: sexual intercourse, sodomy, sexual bestiality, masturbation, sadism, masochism, excretion, or lewd exhibition of the genitals; and

   (c) considered as a whole, it lacks serious literary, artistic, political, and scientific value.

Predominant appeal shall be judged with reference to ordinary adults unless it appears from the character of the material or the circumstances of its dissemination to be designed for children or another specially susceptible audience.

The Degree of Crime

Obscenity was originally a single degree crime under New York law. The crime was later divided into three distinct degrees of offense, the most basic of which is obscenity in the third degree.

Obscenity in the Third Degree - New York Penal Code §235.05

Obscenity in the third degree contains two subdivisions:

Obscene Material

The first part of the statute governs those defendants who promote, or possess with intent to promote, any obscene material. Material is defined as anything tangible which is capable of being used or adapted to arouse interest, whether through the medium of reading, observation, sound or in any other manner.

Simple possession of obscene material is not prohibited under the statute. Nevertheless, if an individual possesses six or more identical or similar obscene articles, he or she is presumed to possess them with intent to promote them.

Obscene Performance

The second part refers to the production of, or the participation in, an obscene performance. Performance is defined as any play, motion picture, dance or other exhibition performed before an audience.

Both the promoter of the obscene performance, and the participant, may be prosecuted under this section.

Obscenity in the Second Degree - New York Penal Code §235.06

If a person has been previously convicted of obscenity in the third degree, a subsequent offense is deemed to be obscenity in the second degree.

Obscenity in the First Degree - New York Penal Code §235.07

Obscenity in the first degree applies to individuals who wholesale promote, or possess with intent to wholesale promote, obscene material. "Wholesale promote" is defined as manufacturing, issuing, selling, providing, mailing, delivering, transferring, transmuting, publishing, distributing, circulating, disseminating, or offering or agreeing to do the same for purposes of resale.

The purpose of this provision is to more strictly punish those who mass produce and distribute obscenity.

Scienter Requirement

The statute requires that the defendant know that the content and the character of the material or performance is obscene. In *People v. Finkelstein*, 9 NY2d 342 (1961), the New York Court of Appeals held that only those who are aware of the obscene character of the material or performance should be punished because it is the *intentional* promotion of obscene materials that the statute seeks to ban.

Nevertheless, possession of obscene materials has been held to permit an inference that the possessor is aware of the content and character of the materials (*People v. Reisman*, 29 NY2d 278 (1971)).

The statute also states that a person who promotes, or intends to promote, obscene material "in the course of business" is presumed to have the requisite culpable mental state.

Defenses to the Crime of Obscenity

The New York Penal Code sets forth two affirmative defenses to the crime of obscenity:

Justified Purpose

The first affirmative defense applies to persons or institutions who have some scientific, educational or governmental purpose for possessing or viewing obscene materials.

Motion Picture Theater Employees

The second affirmative defense applies to certain employees of a motion picture theater who (1) are in a nonsupervisory position; and (2) have no financial interest in promotion or presentation of the obscene material or performance.

Minors

The New York Penal Code at §235.21 prohibits the distribution of indecent material to minors and classifies the crime as an E felony. The statute provides that:

A person is guilty of disseminating indecent material to minors when:

1. With knowledge of its character and content, he sells or loans to a minor for monetary consideration:

(a) Any picture, photograph, drawing, sculpture, motion picture film, or similar visual representation or image of a person or portion of the human body which depicts nudity, sexual conduct or sado-masochistic abuse and which is harmful to minors; or

(b) Any book, pamphlet, magazine, printed matter however reproduced, or sound recording which contains any matter enumerated in paragraph (a) hereof, or explicit and detailed verbal descriptions or narrative accounts of sexual excitement, sexual conduct or sado-masochistic abuse and which, taken as a whole, is harmful to minors; or

2.   Knowing the character and content of a motion picture, show or other presentation which, in whole or in part, depicts nudity, sexual conduct or sado-masochistic abuse, and which is harmful to minors, he:

(a) Exhibits such motion picture, show or other presentation to a minor for a monetary consideration; or

(b) Sells to a minor an admission ticket or pass to premises whereon there is exhibited or to be exhibited such motion picture, show or other presentation; or

(c) Admits a minor for a monetary consideration to premises whereon there is exhibited or to be exhibited such motion picture show or other presentation.

The statute applies to minors less than 17 years old from material or performances which may not be deemed obscene under the law, but which are considered harmful to minors.

The term "harmful to minors" is defined as "that quality of any description or representation, in whatever form, of nudity, sexual conduct, sexual excitement, or sado-masochistic abuse, when it:

1. Considered as a whole, appeals to the prurient interest in sex of minors; and

2. Is patently offensive to prevailing standards in the adult community as a whole with respect to what is suitable for minors; and

3. Considered as a whole, lacks serious literary, artistic, political and scientific value for minors.

Presumption and Defense

Under the statute, an individual who engages in the prohibited conduct is presumed to do so with knowledge of the character and content of the material. An affirmative defense is available to the defendant if:

1. The defendant had reasonable cause to believe that the minor was seventeen years old or more; and

2. The minor provided the defendant with official documentation which showed that the minor was of age, e.g. a birth certificate, drivers license, etc.

Child Pornography

Under §263.00 et. seq. of the New York Penal Code, there are three separate crimes concerning child pornography. They include the following:

1. Use of a Child in a Sexual Performance - New York Penal Code §263.05

An individual is guilty under this section if he or she, with the knowledge of its character and content, employs, authorizes or induces a child under the age of sixteen to engage in a sexual performance. A sexual performance is defined as any performance which includes sexual conduct by a child less than sixteen years of age.

The parent, legal guardian or custodian of the child may also be guilty under the statute if he or she consents to the child's participation. This offense is classified as a C Felony

2. Promoting an Obscene Sexual Performance by a Child - New York Penal Code §263.10

An individual is guilty under this section if he or she, knowing the character and content thereof, produces, directs or promotes any obscene performance which includes sexual conduct by a child less than sixteen years of age. This offense is classified as a D felony.

3. Promoting an Obscene Sexual Performance by a Child -
New York Penal Code §263.15

An individual is guilty under this section if he or she, knowing
the character and content thereof, produces, directs or promotes
any performance which includes sexual conduct by a child less
than sixteen years of age. This offense is classified as a D felony.

Recent case law has held that an individual who possesses child
pornography for personal use is also guilty of promoting an obscene sexual performance by a child under this section (*People v.
Keyes*, 75 N.Y.2d 342 (1990).

The court determined that the term "procure" is included in the
statutory definition of "promote," and further interpreted "procure"
to include the "acquisition of child pornography, whether for personal consumption or for distribution to others."

The court's reasoning is that the statute's intent is to eradicate
child pornography, and is thus directed at the consumers as well as
the manufacturers and distributors.

Affirmative Defenses

The statute provides that an affirmative defense is available to
any defendant who:

1. In good faith, reasonably believed the person
appearing in the performance was sixteen years of age or
older. When the child's age is in issue, a personal
inspection of the child may be undertaken.

2. Worked in a nonsupervisory position and had no
financial interest in the promotion, presentation or
direction of any such sexual performance.

The subject of child pornography is further discussed in Chapter
5.

APPENDICIES

APPENDIX 1:

DIRECTORY OF NATIONAL
ANTI-PORNOGRAPHY ORGANIZATIONS

NAME
ADDRESS
TELEPHONE NUMBER

American Family Association
107 Parkgate
Tupelo, MS 38803
601-844-5036

Citizens for Decency Through Law, Inc.
2845 East Camelback Road, Suite 740
Phoenix, AZ 85016
602-381-1322

Citizens for Media Responsibility
Without Law
P.O. Box 671
Oshkosh, WI 54902

Morality in Media, Inc. and
National Obscenity Law Center
475 Riverside Drive
New York, NY 10015
212-870-3222

National Christian Association
P.O. Box 40945
Washington, DC 20016
202-296-7155

National Coalition Against
Pornography, Inc.
800 Compton Road, Suite 9248
Cincinnati, OH 45231
513-521-6227

National Organization for Women
1401 New York Avenue NW, Suite 800
Washington DC 20005
202-347-2279

Organizing Against Pornography:
A Resource Center for Education
and Action
310 East 38th Street
Minneapolis, MN 55409
612-822-1476

Taskforce on Prostitution and Pornography
P.O. Box 1602
Madison, WI 53701

Women Against Pornography
358 West 47th Street
New York, NY 10036
212-307-5055[1]

---

1   Source: Sourcebook on Pornography, Lexington Books, 1989

APPENDIX 2:

SELECTED EXCERPTS FROM THE ATTORNEY GENERAL'S COMMISSION ON PORNOGRAPHY

PART TWO

SECTION 1.1: THE COMMISSION AND ITS MANDATE

The formal mandate of the Commission is ... to determine the nature, extent, and impact on society of pornography in the United States, and to make specific recommendations to the Attorney General concerning more effective ways in which the spread of pornography could be contained, consistent with constitutional guarantees.

SECTION 3.1: THE PRESUMPTIVE RELEVANCE OF THE FIRST AMENDMENT

The First Amendment to the Constitution of the United States provides quite simply that "Congress shall make no law ... abridging the freedom of speech, or of the press."

Longstanding judicial interpretations make it now clear that this mandate is, because of the Fourteenth Amendment, applicable to the states as well, and make it equally clear that the restrictions of the First Amendment, are applicable to any form of governmental action, and not merely to statutes enacted by a legislative body.

To the extent, therefore, that regulation of pornography constitutes an abridgement of the freedom of speech, or an abridgement of the freedom of the press, it is at least presumptively unconstitutional.

SECTION 3.2: THE FIRST AMENDMENT, THE SUPREME COURT, AND THE REGULATION OF OBSCENITY

[T]he regulation of pornography in light of the constraints of the First Amendment must ... be considered [and] not every use of words, pictures, or a printing press automatically triggers protection by the First Amendment.

As Justice Holmes stated the matter in 1919, "the First Amendment ... cannot have been, and obviously was not, intended to give immunity for every possible use of language."

The Supreme Court made it clear in *Roth* that some materials were themselves outside of the coverage of the First Amendment, and that obscenity, carefully delineated, could be considered as "utterly without redeeming social importance."

As a result, the Court concluded, obscene materials were not the kind of speech or press included within the First Amendment, and could thus be regulated without the kind of overwhelming evidence of harm that would be necessary if materials of this variety were included within the scope of the First Amendment.

Legal obscenity may constitutionally be regulated as long as there exists merely a "rational basis" for the regulation, a standard undoubtedly drastically less stringent than the standard of "clear and present danger" or "compelling interest."

In the final analysis, the effect of *Miller* ... is to limit obscenity prosecutions to "hard core" material devoid of anything except the most explicit and offensive representations of sex.

SECTION 5.1.1: HARM AND REGULATION - THE SCOPE OF OUR INQUIRY

A central part of our mission has been to examine the question whether pornography is harmful. [W]e feel it entirely proper to identify harms that may accompany certain sexually explicit material before and independent of an inquiry into the desirability and constitutionality of regulating even that sexually explicit material that may be harmful.

As a result, our inquiry into harm encompasses much material that may not be legally obscene, and also encompasses much material that would not generally be considered "pornographic" as we use that term here.

SECTION 5.1.2: WHAT COUNTS AS HARM

We think it important, with respect to every area of possible harm, to focus on whether the allegation relates to a harm that comes from the sexually explicit material itself, or whether it occurs as a result of something the material does.

Thus, the analysis of the hypothesis that pornography causes harm must start with the identification of hypothesized harms, proceed to the determination of whether those hypothesized harms are indeed harmful, and then conclude with the examination of whether a causal link exists between the material and the harm.

If sexually explicit material of some variety is causally related to, or increases the incidence of, some behavior that is harmful, then it is safe to conclude that the material is harmful.

SECTION 5.2.1: SEXUALLY VIOLENT MATERIAL

The category of material which most of the evidence has focused on is the category of material featuring actual or unmistakably simulated or unmistakably threatened violence presented in sexually explicit fashion with a predominant focus on the sexually explicit violence.

SECTION 6.6: OBSCENITY AND THE
ELECTRONIC MEDIA

Where legally obscene material is transmitted by radio, television, telephone, or cable, the same legal sanctions are or should be available as are available for any other form of distribution or exhibition.

SECTION 7.1: THE SPECIAL HORROR OF
CHILD PORNOGRAPHY

What is commonly referred to as "child pornography" is not so much a form of pornography as it is a form of sexual exploitation of children. The distinguishing characteristic of child pornography, as generally understood, is that actual children are photographed while engaged in some form of sexual activity, either with adults or other children.

Child pornography necessarily includes the sexual abuse of a real child, and there can be no understanding of the special problem of child pornography until there is understanding of the special way in which child pornography is child abuse.

SECTION 7.4: ENFORCEMENT OF THE
CHILD PORNOGRAPHY LAWS

None of us doubt that child pornography is extraordinarily harmful both to the children involved and to society, that dealing with child pornography in all of its form ought to be treated as a governmental priority of the greatest urgency, and that an aggressive law enforcement effort is an essential part of this urgent governmental priority.

PART THREE

CHAPTER 1: RECOMMENDATIONS

1. Congress should enact a forfeiture statute to reach the proceeds and instruments of any offense committed in violation of the federal obscenity laws.

2. Congress should amend the federal obscenity laws to eliminate the necessity of proving transportation in interstate commerce. A statute should be enacted to only require proof that the distribution of the obscene material "affects" interstate commerce.

3. Congress should enact legislation making it an unfair business practice and an unfair labor practice for any employer to hire individuals to participate in commercial sexual performances.

4. Congress should amend the Mann Act to make its provisions gender neutral.

5. Congress should amend Title 18 of the United States Code to specifically proscribe obscene cable television programming.

6. Congress should enact legislation to prohibit the transmission of obscene material through the telephone or similar common carrier.

7. State legislatures should amend, if necessary, obscenity statutes containing the definitional requirement that material be "utterly without redeeming social value" in order to be obscene to conform with the current standard enunciated by the United States Supreme Court in *Miller v. California*.

8. State legislatures should amend, if necessary, obscenity statutes to eliminate misdemeanor status for second offenses and make any second offense punishable as a felony.

9. State legislatures should enact, if necessary, forfeiture provisions as part of the state obscenity laws.

10. State legislatures should enact a racketeer influenced corrupt organizations (RICO) statute which has obscenity as a predicate act.

11. The Attorney General should direct the United States Attorneys to examine the obscenity problem in their respective districts, identify offenders, initiate investigations, and commence prosecution without further delay.

12. The Attorney General should appoint a high ranking official from the Department of Justice to oversee the creation and operation of an obscenity task force. The task force should consist of special Assistant United

States Attorneys and federal agents who will assist United States Attorneys in the prosecution and investigation of obscenity cases.

13.   The Department of Justice should initiate the creation of an obscenity law enforcement data base which would serve as a resource network for federal, state and local law enforcement agencies.

14.   The United States Attorneys should use law enforcement coordinating committees to coordinate enforcement of the obscenity laws and to maintain surveillance of the nature and extent of the obscenity problem within each district.

15.   The Department of Justice and United States Attorneys should use the Racketeer Influenced Corrupt Organization Act (RICO) as a means of prosecuting major producers and distributors of obscene material.

16.   The Department of Justice should continue to provide the United States Attorneys with training programs on legal and procedural matters related to obscenity cases and also should make such training available to state and local prosecutors.

17.   The United States Attorneys should use all available federal statutes to prosecute obscenity law violations involving cable and satellite television.

18.   State and local prosecutors should prosecute producers of obscene material under existing laws including those prohibiting pandering and other underlying sexual offenses.

19.   State and local prosecutors should examine the obscenity problem in their jurisdiction, identify offenders, initiate investigations, and commence prosecution without further delay.

20. State and local prosecutors should allocate sufficient resources to prosecute obscenity cases.

21. State and local prosecutors should use the bankruptcy laws to collect unpaid fines.

22. State and local prosecutors should use all available statutes to prosecute obscenity violations involving cable and satellite television.

23. State and local prosecutors should enforce existing corporate laws to prevent the formation, use and abuse of shell corporations which serve as a shelter for producers and distributors of obscene material.

24. State and local prosecutors should enforce the alcoholic beverage control laws that prohibit obscenity on licensed premises.

25. Government attorneys, including state and local prosecutors, should enforce all legal remedies authorized by statute.

26. Federal law enforcement agencies should conduct active and thorough investigations of all significant violations of the obscenity laws with interstate dimensions.

27. The Internal Revenue Service should aggressively investigate violations of the tax laws committed by producers and distributors of obscene material.

28. State and local law enforcement agencies should provide the most thorough and up-to-date training for investigators involved in enforcing the obscenity laws.

29. State and local law enforcement agencies should allocate sufficient personnel to conduct intensive and thorough investigations of any violations of the obscenity laws.

30. State and local law enforcement officers should take an active role in the law enforcement coordinating committees.

31. State and local revenue authorities must insure taxes are collected from businesses dealing in obscene materials.

32. State and local public health authorities should investigate conditions with in "adults only" pornographic outlets and arcades and enforce the laws against any health violations found on those premises.

33. Judges should impose substantial periods of incarceration for persons who are repeatedly convicted of obscenity law violations and when appropriate should order payment of restitution to identified victims as part of the sentence.

34. The Federal Communications Commission should use its full regulatory powers and impose appropriate sanctions against providers of obscene dial-a-porn telephone services.

35. The Federal Communications Commission should use its full regulatory powers and impose appropriate sanctions against cable and satellite television programmers who transmit obscene programs.

36. The President's Commission on Uniform Sentencing should consider a provision for a minimum of one year imprisonment for any second or subsequent violation of federal law involving obscene material that depicts adults.

37. Congress should enact legislation requiring producers, retailers, or distributors of sexually explicit visual depictions to maintain records containing consent forms and proof of performers' ages.

38. Congress should enact legislation prohibiting producers of certain sexually explicit visual depictions from using performers under the age of twenty-one.

39. Congress should enact legislation to prohibit the exchange of information concerning child pornography or children to be used in child pornography through computer networks.

40. Congress should amend The Child Protection Act forfeiture section to include a provision which authorizes the Postal Inspection Service to conduct forfeiture actions.

41. Congress should amend 18 U.S.C. §2255 to define the term "visual depiction" and include undeveloped film in that definition.

42. Congress should enact legislation providing financial incentives for the states to initiate task forces on child pornography and related cases.

43. Congress should enact legislation to make the acts of child selling or child purchasing, for the production of sexually explicit visual depictions, a felony.

44. State legislatures should amend, if necessary, child pornography statutes to include forfeiture provisions.

45. State legislatures should amend laws, where necessary, to make the knowing possession of child pornography a felony.

46. State legislatures should amend, if necessary, laws making the sexual abuse of children through the production of sexually explicit visual depictions, a felony.

47. State legislatures should amend, if necessary, to make the conspiracy to produce, distribute, give away or exhibit any sexually explicit visual depictions of children

or exchange or deliver children for such purpose a felony.

48. State legislatures should amend, if necessary, child pornography laws to create an offense for advertising, selling, purchasing, bartering, exchanging, giving or receiving information as to where sexually explicit materials depicting children can be found.

49. State legislatures should enact or amend legislation, where necessary, to   make child selling or child purchasing for the production of sexually explicit visual depictions, a felony.

50. State legislatures should amend laws, where necessary, to make child pornography in the possession of an alleged child sexual abuser which depicts that person engaged in sexual acts with a minor sufficient evidence of child molestation for use in prosecuting that individual whether or not the child involved is found or is able to testify.

51. State legislatures should amend laws, if necessary, to eliminate the requirement that the prosecution identify or produce testimony from the child who is depicted if proof of age can otherwise be established.

52. State legislatures should enact or amend legislation, if necessary, which requires photo finishing laboratories to report suspected child pornography.

53. State legislatures should enact or amend legislation, if necessary, to permit judges to impose a sentence of lifetime probation for convicted child pornographers and related offenders.

54. The State Department, the United States Department of Justice, the United States Custom Service, the United States Postal Inspection Service, the Federal Bureau of Investigation and other federal agencies should continue to work with other nations to detect and intercept child pornography.

55. The United States Department of Justice should direct the law enforcement coordinated committees to form task forces of dedicated and experienced investigators and prosecutors in major regions to combat child pornography.

56. The Department of Justice or other appropriate federal agency should initiate the creation of a data base which would serve as a resource network for federal, state and local law enforcement agencies to send and obtain information regarding child pornography trafficking.

57. Federal law enforcement agencies should develop and maintain continuous training programs for agents in techniques of child pornography investigations.

58. Federal law enforcement agencies should have personnel trained in child pornography investigation and when possible they should form specialized units for child sexual abuse and child pornography investigation.

59. Federal law enforcement agencies should use search warrants in child pornography and related cases expeditiously as a means of gathering evidence and furthering overall investigation efforts in the child pornography area.

60. Federal law enforcement agents should ask the child victim in reported child sexual abuse cases if photographs or films were made of him or her during the course of sexual abuse.

61. The Department of Justice should appoint a national task force to conduct a study of cases throughout the United States reflecting apparent patterns of multi-victim, multi-perpetrator child sexual exploitation.

62. Local law enforcement agencies should participate in the law enforcement coordinating committees to form regional task forces of dedicated and experienced

investigators and prosecutors to combat child pornography.

63. State and local law enforcement agencies should develop and maintain continuous training programs for officers in identification, apprehension, and undercover techniques of child pornography investigations.

64. State and local law enforcement agencies should participate in a national data base established to serve as a center for state and local law enforcement agencies to submit and receive information regarding child pornography trafficking.

65. State and local law enforcement agencies should have personnel trained in child pornography investigation and when possible they should form specialized units for child sexual abuse and child pornography investigations.

66. State and local law enforcement agencies should use search warrants in child sexual exploitation cases expeditiously as a means of gathering evidence and furthering investigation effort in the child pornography area.

67. State and local law enforcement officers should ask the child victim in reported child sexual abuse cases if photographs or films were made of him or her during the course of sexual abuse.

68. The United States Department of Justice should direct United States Attorneys to participate in law enforcement coordinating committee task forces to combat child pornography.

69. Federal, state and local prosecutors should participate in a task force of multi-disciplinary practitioners and develop a protocol for courtroom procedures for child witnesses that would meet constitutional standards.

70. Prosecutors should assist state, local and federal law enforcement agencies to use search warrants in potential child pornography and related child sexual abuse cases.

71. Federal, state and local prosecutors should ask the child victim in reported child sexual abuse cases if photographs or films were made of him or her during the course of sexual abuse.

72. State and local prosecutors should use the vertical prosecution model in child pornography and related cases.

73. Judges and probation officers should receive specific education so that they may investigate, evaluate, sentence and supervise persons convicted of child pornography and related cases appropriately.

74. Judges should impose appropriate periods of incarceration for convicted child pornographers and related offenders.

75. Judges should use, when appropriate, a sentence of lifetime probation for convicted child pornographers.

76. Pre-sentence reports concerning individuals found guilty of violations of child pornography or related laws should be based on sources of information in addition to the offender himself or herself.

77. State and federal correctional facilities should recognize the unique problems of child pornographers and related offenders and designate appropriate programs regarding their incarceration.

78. Federal, state and local judges should participate in a task force of multi-disciplinary practitioners and develop a protocol for courtroom procedures for child witness that would meet constitutional standards.

79. Public and private social service agencies should participate in a task force of multi-disciplinary practitioners and develop a

protocol for courtroom procedures for child witness that would meet constitutional standards.

80. Social, mental health and medical services should be provided for child pornography victims.

81. Local agencies should allocate victims of crimes funds to provide monies for psychiatric evaluation and treatment and medical treatment of child pornography victims and their families.

82. Clinical evaluators should be trained to assist children victimized through the production and use of child pornography more effectively and to better understand adult psychosexual disorders.

83. Behavioral scientists should conduct research to determine the effects of the production of child pornography and the related victimization on children.

84. States should support age appropriate education and prevention programs for parents, teachers and children within public and private school systems to protect children from victimization by child pornographers and child sexual abusers.

85. A multi-media educational campaign should be developed which increases family and community awareness regarding child sexual exploitation through the production and use of child pornography.

86. State, county and municipal governments should facilitate the development of public and private resources for persons who are currently involved in the production or consumption of pornography and wish to discontinue this involvement and for those who suffer mental, physical, educational or employment disabilities as a result of exposure or participation in the production of pornography.

87. Legislatures should conduct hearings and consider legislation recognizing a civil remedy for harms attributable to pornography.

88. "Adults only" pornographic outlet peep show facilities which provide individual booths for viewing should not be equipped with doors. The occupant of the booth should be clearly visible to eliminate a haven for sexual activity.

89. Holes enabling interbooth sexual contact between patrons should be prohibited in the peep show booths.

90. Because of the apparent health hazards posed by the outlet environment generally, and the peep show booth in particular, such facilities should be subject to periodic inspection and licensing by appropriate governmental agents.

91. Any form of indecent act by or among "adults only" pornographic outlet patrons should be unlawful.

92. Access to "adults only" pornographic outlets should be limited to persons over the age of eighteen.

PART FOUR

CHAPTER 1: ADVERSE EFFECTS [as supported
by testimony given before the Commission]

A. PHYSICAL HARM

1. Rape

The Commission received testimony alleging rapes related to pornography.

2. Forced Sexual Performance

During the course of the hearings the Commission received reports from individuals who described situations in which they were forced to engage in certain sexual acts.

3. Battery and Torture

Witnesses who appeared before the Commission and those who submitted statements reported acts of battery and episodes of torture associated with the production or use of pornography.

4. Murder

In addition to the physical harms already mentioned, some evidence was received alleging a connection between murder and pornographic materials.

5. Imprisonment

The Commission received testimony and other evidence from individuals who reported that they had been kidnapped or held captive during the production of pornographic materials.

6. Sexually Transmitted Diseases

Witnesses reported various injuries and diseases associated with the production of pornography. The diseases which were reported included a variety of sexually transmitted diseases.

7. Masochistic Self Harm

One person described her son's use of pornography and his resulting death.

8. Prostitution

Witnesses who testified before the Commission and individuals who submitted statements reported several connections between pornography and prostitution.

B. PSYCHOLOGICAL HARM

1. Suicidal Thoughts and Behavior

The Commission received testimony from many individuals who reported suicidal thoughts and behavior. These individual described experiences related to pornographic materials that led them to feel worthless and hopeless, which in turn led to thoughts of suicide or attempts.

2. Fear and Anxiety Caused by Seeing Pornography

The Commission heard testimony from several witnesses who described fear and anxiety associated with being shown pornography. The anxieties which have been described may be divided into two primary categories: anxiety attributable to memories of prior abuse which are relived through the images portrayed in the pornography being shown; and an overall embarrassment or discomfort in being made to view pornographic materials.

3. Feelings of Shame and Guilt

The Commission heard testimony from many witnesses who described feelings of worthlessness, guilt and shame which they attributed to experiences involving pornographic materials.

4. Fear of Exposure through Publication or Display of Pornographic Materials

Some witnesses feared the future dissemination of pornography which had been made of them.

5. Amnesia and Denial and Repression of Abuse

The Commission heard accounts from several witnesses who were unable to recall portions of their lives or specific events. These witnesses attributed their amnesia to trauma associated with the production or use of pornography.

6. Nightmares

The mother of an adolescent girl who said she had been sexually abused through the use of pornography testified that her daughter had recurrent nightmares of the abuse.

7. Compulsive Reenactment of Sexual Abuse and Inability to Feel Sexual Pleasure Outside of a Context of Dominance and Submission

Many witnesses described an inability to engage in healthy sexual relationships, including reports of a seeming need for abuse or unhealthy dominance.

8. Inability to Experience Sexual Pleasure and Feelings of Sexual Inadequacy

[W]itnesses attributed feelings of sexual insecurity and inadequacy to experiences with pornography.

9. Feelings of Inferiority and Degradation

Some individuals described situations in which pornography had been used to instill feelings of racial inferiority. Witnesses also described the pornography was used to degrade them as women.

10. Feelings of Frustration with the Legal System

The Commission heard testimony describing feelings of frustration and problems with the legal system. Some of the witnesses described helplessness and frustration which they thought could have been alleviated if they had been provided guidance in seeking legal redress.

11. Abuse of Alcohol and Other Drugs

Several of the witnesses reported the use of various drugs, including alcohol, in connection with the manufacture of pornographic materials.

C. SOCIAL HARMS

1. Loss of Job or Promotion/Sexual Harassment

Reports of sexual harassment similar to those described in the "Physical Injuries" section were also submitted as forms of social injuries. The witnesses stated the harassment was attributable to the presence of pornographic materials and served to reduce their social status.

2. Financial Losses

The Commission heard reports from individuals who encounter financial consequences attributable to experiences with pornography. Many of these witnesses stated they had suffered financial difficulty because of the need to seek medical and mental assistance because of injuries they attributed to pornographic materials.

3. Defamation and Loss of Status in the Community

The Commission received testimony from witnesses who reported that pornographic materials were used to place them in a bad light. The witnesses stated that they had been depicted in pornography without knowledge or consent.

4. Promotion of Racial Hatred

The Commission received statements identifying pornography as a tool to promote racial bias and hatred. Witnesses identified specific pornographic materials which portray persons of color in a derogatory manner. These individuals attributed continued stereotyping and feelings of racial inferiority to the pornographic materials.

5. Loss of Trust Within a Family

The Commission heard reports of family problems attributed to pornography that were more subtle than some of the massive family ruptures described earlier in this Chapter. Some individuals stated that when a family member used pornography or was subjected to the use of pornography, other members of the family felt the effects.

6. Prostitution

Witnesses who testified before the Commission and individuals who submitted statements reported several connections between pornography and prostitution. One such connection was the use of pornography as instructional manuals for prostitutes. Another connection was the use of pornographic films by pimps to blackmail the participants. Yet another connection was the use of magazines to stimulate the clientele. Women who are of who have been prostitutes identified pornography as a significant factor in prostitution. These individuals reported that pornography was not only used and made of them while engaged in acts of prostitution, but they stated that pornography is used to perpetuate the concept that women are accustomed to being placed in the role of a prostitute.

7. Sexual Harassment in the Workplace

Several women reported incidents of sexual harassment in the workplace involving the display and use of pornography.

PART THREE

CHAPTER 2: THE USE OF PERFORMERS IN COMMERCIAL PORNOGRAPHY

SECTION B: THE EVIDENCE

2(a). Age

Perhaps the single most common feature of models is their relative, and in the vast majority of cases, absolute youth.

2(b). Personal Background

Along with their youth, models in sexually explicit media seem to s hare troubled or at least ambivalent personal backgrounds.

2(c). Economic Circumstances

It ... seems clear what chiefly motivates their decision to appear in sexually explicit material: financial need.

3(a). Recruitment

For most young women in commercial pornography, entry into "modeling" seems to occur almost without serious thought.

3(b). Coercion

It is an unpleasant, controversial, but in our view well established fact, that at least some performers have been physically coerced into appearing in sexually explicit material, while others have been forced to engage in sexual activity during performances that they had not agreed to beforehand.

3(e). Health Risks

Precisely because sex is their job, models face health hazards of forbidding intensity.

3(f). Drug Use

Along with the insidious threat of infectious disease, models face a more overt challenge to their physical health: drug use, and in particular, use of cocaine.[1].

---

[1]   Source: Attorney General's Commission on Pornography, U.S. Department of Justice, 1986

APPENDIX 3:

THE COMMUNICATIONS DECENCY ACT OF 1996

THE COMMUNICATIONS DECENCY ACT OF 1996

TITLE V OF THE TELECOMMUNICATIONS ACT OF 1996 - OBSCENITY AND VIOLENCE

SUBTITLE A: OBSCENE, HARASSING, WRONGFUL UTILIZATION OF TELECOMMUNICATIONS FACILITIES

SECTION 501. SHORT TITLE.

This title may be cited as the "Communications Decency Act of 1996".

SECTION 502. OBSCENE OR HARASSING USE OF TELECOMMUNICATIONS FACILITIES UNDER THE COMMUNICATIONS ACT OF 1934.

SECTION 223 (47 U.S.C. 223) is amended—

(1) by striking subsection (a) and inserting in lieu thereof:

(a) Whoever—

(1) in interstate or foreign communications

(A) by means of a telecommunications device knowingly

(i) makes, creates, or solicits, and

(ii) initiates the transmission of, any comment, request, suggestion, proposal, image, or other communication which is obscene, lewd, lascivious, filthy, or indecent, with intent to annoy, abuse, threaten, or harass another person;

(B) by means of a telecommunications device knowingly—

(i) makes, creates, or solicits, and

(ii) initiates the transmission of, any comment, request, suggestion, proposal, image, or other communication which is obscene or indecent, knowing that the recipient of the communication is under 18 years of age, regardless of whether the maker of such communication placed the call or initiated the communication;

(C) makes a telephone call or utilizes a telecommunications device, whether or not conversation or communication ensues, without disclosing his identity and with intent to annoy, abuse, threaten, or harass any person at the called number or who receives the communications;

(D) makes or causes the telephone of another repeatedly or continuously to ring, with intent to harass any person at the called number; or

(E) makes repeated telephone calls or repeatedly initiates communication with a telecommunications device, during which conversation or communication ensues, solely to harass any person at the called number or who receives the communication; or

(2) knowingly permits any telecommunications facility under his control to be used for any activity prohibited by paragraph (1) with the intent that it be used for such activity, shall be fined under title 18, United States Code, or imprisoned not more than two years, or both."; and

(2) by adding at the end the following new subsections:

(d) Whoever—

(1) in interstate or foreign communications knowingly—

(A) uses an interactive computer service to send to a specific person or persons under 18 years of age, or

(B) uses any interactive computer service to display in a manner available to a person under 18 years of age, any comment, request, suggestion, proposal, image, or other communication that, in context, depicts or describes, in terms patently offensive as measured by contemporary community standards, sexual or excretory activities or organs, regardless of whether the user of such service placed the call or initiated the communication; or

(2) knowingly permits any telecommunications facility under such person's control to be used for an activity prohibited by paragraph (1) with the intent that it be used for such activity, shall be fined under title 18, United States Code, or imprisoned not more than two years, or both.

(e) In addition to any other defenses available by law:

(1) No person shall be held to have violated subsection (a) or (d) solely for providing access or connection to or from a facility, system, or network not under that person's control, including transmission, downloading, intermediate storage, access software, or other related capabilities that are incidental to providing such access or connection that does not include the creation of the content of the communication.

(2) The defenses provided by paragraph (1) of this subsection shall not be applicable to a person who is a conspirator with an entity actively involved in the creation or knowing distribution of communications that violate this section, or who knowingly advertises the availability of such communications.

(3) The defenses provided in paragraph (1) of this subsection shall not be applicable to a person who provides access or connection to a facility, system, or network engaged in the violation of this section that is owned or controlled by such person.

(4) No employer shall be held liable under this section for the actions of an employee or agent unless the employee's or agent's conduct is within the scope of his or her employment or agency and the employer

(A) having knowledge of such conduct, authorizes or ratifies such conduct, or

(B) recklessly disregards such conduct.

(5) It is a defense to a prosecution under subsection (a)(1)(B) or (d), or under subsection (a)(2) with respect to the use of a facility for an activity under subsection (a)(1)(B) that a person—

(A) has taken, in good faith, reasonable, effective, and appropriate actions under the circumstances to restrict or prevent access by minors to a communication specified in such subsections, which may involve any appropriate measures to restrict minors from such communications, including any method which is feasible under available technology; or

(B) has restricted access to such communication by requiring use of a verified credit card, debit account, adult access code, or adult personal identification number.

(6) The Commission may describe measures which are reasonable, effective, and appropriate to restrict access to prohibited communications under subsection (d). Nothing in this section authorizes the Commission to enforce, or is intended to provide the Commission with the authority to approve, sanction, or permit, the use of such measures. The Commission shall have no enforcement authority over the failure to utilize such measures. The Commission shall not endorse specific products relating to such measures. The use of such measures shall be admitted as evidence of good faith efforts for purposes of paragraph (5) in any action arising under subsection (d). Nothing in this section shall be construed to treat interactive computer

services as common carriers or telecommunications carriers.

(f)(1) No cause of action may be brought in any court or administrative agency against any person on account of any activity that is not in violation of any law punishable by criminal or civil penalty, and that the person has taken in good faith to implement a defense authorized under this section or otherwise to restrict or prevent the transmission of, or access to, a communication specified in this section.

(2) No State or local government may impose any liability for commercial activities or actions by commercial entities, nonprofit libraries, or institutions of higher education in connection with an activity or action described in subsection (a)(2) or (d) that is inconsistent with the treatment of those activities or actions under this section: Provided, however, That nothing herein shall preclude any State or local government from enacting and enforcing complementary oversight, liability, and regulatory systems, procedures, and requirements, so long as such systems, procedures, and requirements govern only intrastate services and do not result in the imposition of inconsistent rights, duties or obligations on the provision of interstate services. Nothing in this subsection shall preclude any State or local government from governing conduct not covered by this section.

(g) Nothing in subsection (a), (d), (e), or (f) or in the defenses to prosecution under subsection (a) or (d) shall be construed to affect or limit the application or enforcement of any other Federal law.

(h) For purposes of this section—

(1) The use of the term 'telecommunications device' in this section—

(A) shall not impose new obligations on broadcasting station licensees and cable operators covered by obscenity and indecency provisions elsewhere in this Act; and

(B) does not include an interactive computer service.

(2) The term 'interactive computer service' has the meaning provided in section 230(e)(2).

(3) The term 'access software' means software (including client or server software) or enabling tools that do not create or provide the content of the communication but that allow a user to do any one or more of the following:

(A) filter, screen, allow, or disallow content;

(B) pick, choose, analyze, or digest content; or

(C) transmit, receive, display, forward, cache, search, subset, organize, reorganize, or translate content.

(4) The term 'institution of higher education' has the meaning provided in section 1201 of the Higher Education Act of 1965 (20 U.S.C. 1141).

(5) The term 'library' means a library eligible for participation in State-based plans for funds under title III of the Library Services and Construction Act (20 U.S.C. 355e et seq.).".

SECTION 503. OBSCENE PROGRAMMING ON CABLE TELEVISION.

Section 639 (47 U.S.C. 559) is amended by striking "not more than $ 10,000" and inserting "under title 18, United States Code,".

SECTION 504. SCRAMBLING OF CABLE CHANNELS FOR NONSUBSCRIBERS.

Part IV of title VI (47 U.S.C. 551 et seq.) is amended by adding at the end the following:

SECTION 640. SCRAMBLING OF CABLE CHANNELS
FOR NONSUBSCRIBERS.

(a) Subscriber Request.—Upon request by a cable service subscriber, a cable operator shall, without charge, fully scramble or
otherwise fully block the audio and video programming of each
channel carrying such programming so that a subscriber does not
receive it.

(b) Definition.—As used in this section, the term 'scramble'
means to rearrange the content of the signal of the programming so
that the programming cannot be viewed or heard in an understandable manner.".

SECTION 505. SCRAMBLING OF SEXUALLY
EXPLICIT ADULT VIDEO
SERVICE PROGRAMMING.

(a) Requirement.—Part IV of title VI (47 U.S.C. 551 et seq.), as
amended by this Act, is further amended by adding at the end the
following:

SECTION 641. SCRAMBLING OF SEXUALLY EXPLICIT
ADULT VIDEO SERVICE PROGRAMMING.

(a) Requirement.—In providing sexually explicit adult programming or other programming that is indecent on any channel of its
service primarily dedicated to sexually-oriented programming, a
multichannel video programming distributor shall fully scramble or
otherwise fully block the video and audio portion of such channel
so that one not a subscriber to such channel or programming does
not receive it.

(b) Implementation.—Until a multichannel video programming
distributor complies with the requirement set forth in subsection
(a), the distributor shall limit the access of children to the programming referred to in that subsection by not providing such programming during the hours of the day (as determined by the

Commission) when a significant number of children are likely to view it.

(c) Definition.—As used in this section, the term 'scramble' means to rearrange the content of the signal of the programming so that the programming cannot be viewed or heard in an understandable manner".

(b) Effective Date.—The amendment made by subsection (a) shall take effect 30 days after the date of enactment of this Act.

SECTION 506. CABLE OPERATOR REFUSAL TO CARRY CERTAIN PROGRAMS.

(a) Public, Educational, and Governmental Channels.—Section 611(e) (47 U.S.C. 531(e)) is amended by inserting before the period the following: ", except a cable operator may refuse to transmit any public access program or portion of a public access program which contains obscenity, indecency, or nudity".

(b) Cable Channels for Commercial Use.—Section 612(c)(2) (47 U.S.C. 532(c)(2)) is amended by striking "an operator" and inserting "a cable operator may refuse to transmit any leased access program or portion of a leased access program which contains obscenity, indecency, or nudity and".

SECTION 507. CLARIFICATION OF CURRENT LAWS REGARDING COMMUNICATION OF OBSCENE MATERIALS THROUGH THE USE OF COMPUTERS.

(a) Importation or Transportation.—Section 1462 of title 18, United States Code, is amended—

(1) in the first undesignated paragraph, by inserting "or interactive computer service (as defined in section 230(e)(2) of the Communications Act of 1934)" after "carrier"; and

(2) in the second undesignated paragraph—

(A) by inserting "or receives," after "takes";

(B) by inserting "or interactive computer service (as defined in section 230(e)(2) of the Communications Act of 1934)" after "common carrier"; and

(C) by inserting "or importation" after "carriage".

(b) Transportation for Purposes of Sale or Distribution.—The first undesignated paragraph of section 1465 of title 18, United States Code, is amended—

(1) by striking "transports in" and inserting "transports or travels in, or uses a facility or means of";

(2) by inserting "or an interactive computer service (as defined in section 230(e)(2) of the Communications Act of 1934) in or affecting such commerce" after "foreign commerce" the first place it appears;

(3) by striking ", or knowingly travels in" and all that follows through "obscene material in interstate or foreign commerce," and inserting "of".

(c) Interpretation.—The amendments made by this section are clarifying and shall not be interpreted to limit or repeal any prohibition contained in sections 1462 and 1465 of title 18, United States Code, before such amendment, under the rule established in United States v. Alpers, 338 U.S. 680 (1950).

Section 508. COERCION AND ENTICEMENT OF MINORS.

Section 2422 of title 18, United States Code, is amended—

(1) by inserting "(a)" before "Whoever knowingly"; and

(2) by adding at the end the following: (b) Whoever, using any facility or means of interstate or foreign commerce, including the mail, or within the special maritime and territorial jurisdiction of the United

States, knowingly persuades, induces, entices, or coerces any individual who has not attained the age of 18 years to engage in prostitution or any sexual act for which any person may be criminally prosecuted, or attempts to do so, shall be fined under this title or imprisoned not more than 10 years, or both.".

SECTION 509. ONLINE FAMILY EMPOWERMENT.

Title II of the Communications Act of 1934 (47 U.S.C. 201 et seq.) is amended by adding at the end the following new section:

SECTION 230. PROTECTION FOR PRIVATE BLOCKING AND SCREENING OF OFFENSIVE MATERIAL.

(a) Findings.—The Congress finds the following:

(1) The rapidly developing array of Internet and other interactive computer services available to individual Americans represent an extraordinary advance in the availability of educational and informational resources to our citizens.

(2) These services offer users a great degree of control over the information that they receive, as well as the potential for even greater control in the future as technology develops.

(3) The Internet and other interactive computer services offer a forum for a true diversity of political discourse, unique opportunities for cultural development, and myriad avenues for intellectual activity.

(4) The Internet and other interactive computer services have flourished, to the benefit of all Americans, with a minimum of government regulation.

(5) Increasingly Americans are relying on interactive media for a variety of political, educational, cultural, and entertainment services.

(b) Policy.—It is the policy of the United States—

(1) to promote the continued development of the Internet and other interactive computer services and other interactive media;

(2) to preserve the vibrant and competitive free market that presently exists for the Internet and other interactive computer services, unfettered by Federal or State regulation;

(3) to encourage the development of technologies which maximize user control over what information is received by individuals, families, and schools who use the Internet and other interactive computer services;

(4) to remove disincentives for the development and utilization of blocking and filtering technologies that empower parents to restrict their children's access to objectionable or inappropriate online material; and

(5) to ensure vigorous enforcement of Federal criminal laws to deter and punish trafficking in obscenity, stalking, and harassment by means of computer.

(c) Protection for 'Good Samaritan' Blocking and Screening of Offensive Material.—

(1) Treatment of publisher or speaker.— No provider or user of an interactive computer service shall be treated as the publisher or speaker of any information provided by another information content provider.

(2) Civil liability.— No provider or user of an interactive computer service shall be held liable on account of—

(A) any action voluntarily taken in good faith to restrict access to or availability of material that the provider or user considers to be obscene, lewd, lascivious, filthy, excessively violent, harassing, or otherwise objectionable, whether or not such material is constitutionally protected; or

(B) any action taken to enable or make available to information content providers or others the technical means to restrict access to material described in paragraph (1).

(d) Effect on Other Laws.—

(1) No effect on criminal law.— Nothing in this section shall be construed to impair the enforcement of section 223 of this Act, chapter 71 (relating to obscenity) or 110 (relating to sexual exploitation of children) of title 18, United States Code, or any other Federal criminal statute.

(2) No effect on intellectual property law.— Nothing in this section shall be construed to limit or expand any law pertaining to intellectual property.

(3) State law.— Nothing in this section shall be construed to prevent any State from enforcing any State law that is consistent with this section. No cause of action may be brought and no liability may be imposed under any State or local law that is inconsistent with this section.

(4) No effect on communications privacy law.— Nothing in this section shall be construed to limit the application of the Electronic Communications Privacy Act of 1986 or any of the amendments made by such Act, or any similar State law.

(e) Definitions.—As used in this section:

(1) Internet.— The term 'Internet' means the international computer network of both Federal and non-Federal interoperable packet switched data networks.

(2) Interactive computer service.— The term 'interactive computer service' means any information service, system, or access software provider that provides or enables computer access by multiple users

to a computer server, including specifically a service or system that provides access to the Internet and such systems operated or services offered by libraries or educational institutions.

(3) Information content provider.— The term 'information content provider' means any person or entity that is responsible, in whole or in part, for the creation or development of information provided through the Internet or any other interactive computer service.

(4) Access software provider.— The term 'access software provider' means a provider of software (including client or server software), or enabling tools that do any one or more of the following:

(A) filter, screen, allow, or disallow content;

(B) pick, choose, analyze, or digest content; or

(C) transmit, receive, display, forward, cache, search, subset, organize, reorganize, or translate content.".

SUBTITLE B: VIOLENCE

SECTION 551. PARENTAL CHOICE IN TELEVISION PROGRAMMING.

(a) Findings.—The Congress makes the following findings:

(1) Television influences children's perception of the values and behavior that are common and acceptable in society.

(2) Television station operators, cable television system operators, and video programmers should follow practices in connection with video programming that take into consideration that television broadcast and cable programming has established a uniquely pervasive presence in the lives of American children.

(3) The average American child is exposed to 25 hours of television each week and some children are exposed to as much as 11 hours of television a day.

(4) Studies have shown that children exposed to violent video programming at a young age have a higher tendency for violent and aggressive behavior later in life than children not so exposed, and that children exposed to violent video programming are prone to assume that acts of violence are acceptable behavior.

(5) Children in the United States are, on average, exposed to an estimated 8,000 murders and 100,000 acts of violence on television by the time the child completes elementary school.

(6) Studies indicate that children are affected by the pervasiveness and casual treatment of sexual material on television, eroding the ability of parents to develop responsible attitudes and behavior in their children.

(7) Parents express grave concern over violent and sexual video programming and strongly support technology that would give them greater control to block video programming in the home that they consider harmful to their children.

(8) There is a compelling governmental interest in empowering parents to limit the negative influences of video programming that is harmful to children.

(9) Providing parents with timely information about the nature of upcoming video programming and with the technological tools that allow them easily to block violent, sexual, or other programming that they believe harmful to their children is a nonintrusive and narrowly tailored means of achieving that compelling governmental interest.

(b) Establishment of Television Rating Code.—

(1) Amendment.— Section 303 (47 U.S.C. 303) is amended by adding at the end the following:

(w) Prescribe—

(1) on the basis of recommendations from an advisory committee established by the Commission in accordance with section 551(b)(2) of the Telecommunications Act of 1996, guidelines and recommended procedures for the identification and rating of video programming that contains sexual, violent, or other indecent material about which parents should be informed before it is displayed to children: Provided, That nothing in this paragraph shall be construed to authorize any rating of video programming on the basis of its political or religious content; and

(2) with respect to any video programming that has been rated, and in consultation with the television industry, rules requiring distributors of such video programming to transmit such rating to permit parents to block the display of video programming that they have determined is inappropriate for their children.".

(2) Advisory committee requirements.— In establishing an advisory committee for purposes of the amendment made by paragraph (1) of this subsection, the Commission shall—

(A) ensure that such committee is composed of parents, television broadcasters, television programming producers, cable operators, appropriate public interest groups, and other interested individuals from the private sector and is fairly balanced in terms of political affiliation, the points of view represented, and the functions to be performed by the committee;

(B) provide to the committee such staff and resources as may be necessary to permit it to perform its functions efficiently and promptly; and

(C) require the committee to submit a final report of its recommendations within one year after the date of the appointment of the initial members.

(c) Requirement for Manufacture of Televisions That Block Programs.—Section 303 (47 U.S.C. 303), as amended by subsection (a), is further amended by adding at the end the following:

> (x) Require, in the case of an apparatus designed to receive television signals that are shipped in interstate commerce or manufactured in the United States and that have a picture screen 13 inches or greater in size (measured diagonally), that such apparatus be equipped with a feature designed to enable viewers to block display of all programs with a common rating, except as otherwise permitted by

(d) Shipping of Televisions That Block Programs.—

> (1) Regulations.— Section 330 (47 U.S.C. 330) is amended—
>
> > (A) by redesignating subsection (c) as subsection (d); and
> >
> > (B) by adding after subsection (b) the following new subsection (c):
>
> (c)(1) Except as provided in paragraph (2), no person shall ship in interstate commerce or manufacture in the United States any apparatus described in section 303(x) of this Act except in accordance with rules prescribed by the Commission pursuant to the authority granted by that section.
>
> (c)(2) This subsection shall not apply to carriers transporting apparatus referred to in paragraph (1) without trading in it.
>
> (c)(3) The rules prescribed by the Commission under this subsection shall provide for the oversight by the Commission of the adoption of standards by industry for blocking technology. Such rules shall require that all such apparatus be able to receive the rating signals which have been transmitted by way of line 21 of the vertical blanking interval and which conform to the

signal and blocking specifications established by industry under the supervision of the Commission.

(c)(4) As new video technology is developed, the Commission shall take such action as the Commission determines appropriate to ensure that blocking service continues to be available to consumers. If the Commission determines that an alternative blocking technology exists that—

(A) enables parents to block programming based on identifying programs without ratings,

(B) is available to consumers at a cost which is comparable to the cost of technology that allows parents to block programming based on common ratings, and

(C) will allow parents to block a broad range of programs on a multichannel system as effectively and as easily as technology that allows parents to block programming based on common ratings, the Commission shall amend the rules prescribed pursuant to section 303(x) to require that the apparatus described in such section be equipped with either the blocking technology described in such section or the alternative blocking technology described in this paragraph.".

(2) Conforming amendment.— Section 330(d), as redesignated by subsection (d)(1)(A), is amended by striking "section 303(s), and section 303(u)" and inserting in lieu thereof "and sections 303(s), 303(u), and 303(x)".

(e) Applicability and Effective Dates.—

(1) Applicability of rating provision.— The amendment made by subsection (b) of this section shall take effect 1 year after the date of enactment of this Act, but only if the Commission determines, in consultation with appropriate public interest groups and interested individuals from the that distributors of video programming have not, by such date—

(A) established voluntary rules for rating video programming that contains sexual, violent, or other indecent material about which parents should be informed before it is displayed to children, and such rules are acceptable to the Commission; and

(B) agreed voluntarily to broadcast signals that contain ratings of such programming.

(2) Effective date of manufacturing provision.— In prescribing regulations to implement the amendment made by subsection (c), the Federal Communications Commission shall, after consultation with the television manufacturing industry, specify the effective date for the applicability of the requirement to the apparatus covered by such amendment, which date shall not be less than two years after the date of enactment of this Act.

SECTION 552. TECHNOLOGY FUND.

It is the policy of the United States to encourage broadcast television, cable, satellite, syndication, other video programming distributors, and relevant related industries (in consultation with appropriate public interest groups and interested individuals from the private sector) to—

(1) establish a technology fund to encourage television and electronics equipment manufacturers to facilitate the development of technology which would empower parents to block programming they deem inappropriate for their children and to encourage the availability thereof to low income parents;

(2) report to the viewing public on the status of the development of affordable, easy to use blocking technology; and

(3) establish and promote effective procedures, standards, systems, advisories, or other mechanisms for ensuring that users have easy and complete access to the information necessary to effectively utilize blocking technology

and to encourage the availability thereof to low income parents.

SUBTITLE C: JUDICIAL REVIEW

SECTION 561. EXPEDITED REVIEW.

(a) Three-Judge District Court Hearing.—Notwithstanding any other provision of law, any civil action challenging the constitutionality, on its face, of this title or any amendment made by this title, or any provision thereof, shall be heard by a district court of 3 judges convened pursuant to the provisions of section 2284 of title 28, United States Code.

(b) Appellate Review.—Notwithstanding any other provision of law, an interlocutory or final judgment, decree, or order of the court of 3 judges in an action under subsection (a) holding this title or an amendment made by this title, or any provision thereof, unconstitutional shall be reviewable as a matter of right by direct appeal to the Supreme Court. Any such appeal shall be filed not more than 20 days after entry of such judgment, decree, or order.

APPENDIX 4:

TABLE OF STATE CHILD PORNOGRAPHY STATUTES

STATE	STATUTE
Alabama	Code of Alabama, § 13-A-12-190, et. seq.
Alaska	Alaska Statutes, §11.41.455; 11.61.125
Arizona	Arizona Revised Statutes Annotated, §13-3552, et. seq
Arkansas	Arkansas Statutes Annotated, § 41-4203, et. seq.
California	California Penal Code, § 311.2, et. seq.
Colorado	§18-6-403, et. seq.
Connecticut	Connecticut General Statutes Annotated, § 53a-196a; 196b
Delaware	Delaware Code Annotated, Title 11, §1108
District of Columbia	District of Columbia Code, § 22-2011, et. seq.
Florida	Florida Statutes Annotated, § 827.071
Georgia	Code of Georgia, § 26-9943a
Hawaii	Hawaii Revised Statutes, § 707-750; 751
Idaho	Idaho Labor Code, §18-1507
Illinois	Illinois Revised Statutes, Chapter 38, §11-20.1; § 3-6(c)
Indiana	Indiana Code Annotated, § 35-42-4-4

Iowa	Code of Iowa, § 728.12
Kansas	Kansas Statutes Annotated, § 21-3516
Kentucky	Kentucky Revised Statutes, § 531.300, et. seq.
Louisiana	Louisiana Revised Statutes, § 14:81.1
Maine	Maine Revised Statutes Annotated, Title 17, § 2921, et. seq.
Maryland	Maryland Annotated Code, Article 27, § 419A
Massachusetts	Massachusetts Annotated Laws, Chapter 272, § 29A, et. seq.
Michigan	Michigan Statutes Annotated, § 750.145c
Minnesota	Minnesota Statutes Annotated, § 617.246, et. seq.
Mississippi	Mississippi Code Annotated, § 97-5-31, et. seq
Missouri	Annotated Missouri Statutes, § 568.06, et. seq
Montana	Revised Montana Code Annotated, § 45-5-625
Nebraska	Nebraska Revised Statutes, § 28-1463, et. seq.
New Hampshire	New Hampshire Revised Statutes Annotated, § 649-A
New Jersey	New Jersey Revised Statutes Annotated, § 2C: 24-4
New Mexico	New Mexico Statutes Annotated, § 0-6A-1, et. seq

New York	New York Penal Law, § 263.00, et. seq.
North Carolina	General Statutes of North Carolina, § 14.190.13, et. seq.
North Dakota	North Dakota Century Code, § 12.1-27.2-01, et. seq.
Ohio	Ohio Revised Code Annotated, § 2907. 321, et. seq
Oklahoma	Oklahoma Statutes Annotated, Title 21, § 1021.2, et. seq
Oregon	Oregon Revised Statutes, § 163.483, et. seq.
Pennsylvania	Title 18, § 6312
Rhode Island	Rhode Island General Laws, § 11-9-1
South Carolina	South Carolina Code Annotated, § 22-22-22, et. seq
Tennessee	Tennessee Code Annotated, § 39-6-1137, et. seq
Texas	Texas Penal Code, § 43.25, et. seq
Utah	Utah Code Annotated, § 76-5a-1, et. seq
Vermont	Title 13, § 2821, et. seq.
Virginia	Code of Virginia Annotated, § 18.2-374.1
Washington	Washington Revised Code, § 9.68A.040, et. seq
West Virginia	West Virginia Code, § 161-8C-1, et. seq
Wisconsin	Wisconsin Statutes Annotated, § 940.203
Wyoming	Wyoming Statutes, § 6-4-403

GLOSSARY

GLOSSARY

Action at Law - A judicial proceeding whereby one party prosecutes another for a wrong done.

Actionable - Giving rise to a cause of action.

Admissible Evidence - Evidence which may be received by a trial court to assist the trier of fact, either the judge or jury, in deciding a dispute.

Admission - In criminal law, the voluntary acknowledgment that certain facts are true.

Affirmative Defense - In a pleading, a matter constituting a defense.

American Civil Liberties Union (ACLU) - A nationwide organization dedicated to the enforcement and preservation of rights and civil liberties guaranteed by the federal and state constitutions.

Answer - In a civil proceeding, the principal pleading on the part of the defendant in response to the plaintiff's complaint.

Appeal - Resort to a higher court for the purpose of obtaining a review of a lower court decision.

Appearance - To come into court, personally or through an attorney, after being summoned.

Appellate Court - A court having jurisdiction to review the law as applied to a prior determination of the same case.

Arguendo - A position taken for the sake of argument even if that position is later contradicted.

Argument - A discourse set forth for the purpose of establishing one's position in a controversy.

Arraign - In a criminal proceeding, to accuse one of committing a wrong.

Arraignment - The initial step in the criminal process when the defendant is formally charged with the wrongful conduct.

Arrest - To deprive a person of his liberty by legal authority.

Bestiality - The illegal act of sexual intercourse with an animal.

Bill of Rights - The first eight amendments to the United States Constitution.

Burden of Proof - The duty of a party to substantiate an allegation or issue to convince the trier of fact as to the truth of their claim.

Capacity - Capacity is the legal qualification concerning the ability of one to understand the nature and effects of one's acts.

Cause of Action - The factual basis for bringing a lawsuit.

Censorship - Review of publications, movies, plays and the like for the purpose of prohibiting the publication, distribution or production of material deemed objectionable as obscene, indecent or immoral.

Certiorari - A common law writ whereby a higher court requests a review of a lower court's records to determine whether any irregularities occurred in a particular proceeding.

Chief Justice - The presiding member of certain courts which have more than one judge, e.g., the United States Supreme Court.

Child Abuse - Any form of cruelty to a child's physical, moral or mental well-being.

Child Welfare - A generic term which embraces the totality of measures necessary for a child's well being; physical, moral and mental.

Circuit - A judicial division of a state or the United States.

Circuit Court - One of several courts in a given jurisdiction.

Circumstantial Evidence - Indirect evidence by which a principal fact may be inferred.

Citation - A reference to a source of legal authority, such as a case or statute.

Conclusion of Fact - A conclusion reached by natural inference and based solely on the facts presented.

Conclusion of Law - A conclusion reached through the application of rules of law.

Conclusive Evidence - Evidence which is incontrovertible.

Concurrent - In criminal law, refers to sentences which are to be served simultaneously.

Confession In criminal law, an admission of guilt or other incriminating statement made by the accused.

Confrontation Clause - A Sixth Amendment right of the Constitution which permits the accused in a criminal prosecution to confront the witness against him.

Consent Search - A search which is carried out with the voluntary authorization of the subject of the search.

Consequential Damages - Consequential damages are those damages which are caused by an injury, but which are not a necessary result of the injury, and must be specially pleaded and proven in order to be awarded.

Conspiracy - A scheme by two or more persons to commit a criminal or unlawful act.

Conspirator - One of the parties involved in a conspiracy.

Constitution - The fundamental principles of law which frame a governmental system.

Constitutional Right - Refers to the individual liberties granted by the constitution of a state or the federal government.

Court - The branch of government responsible for the resolution of disputes arising under the laws of the government.

Criminal Court - The court designed to hear prosecutions under the criminal laws.

Cross-Examination - The questioning of a witness by someone other than the one who called the witness to the stand concerning matters about which the witness testified during direct examination.

Culpable - Referring to conduct, it is that which is deserving of moral blame.

Defamation - The publication of an injurious statement about the reputation of another.

Defendant - In a civil proceeding, the party responding to the complaint.

Defense - Opposition to the truth or validity of the plaintiff's claims.

Delinquent - An infant of not more than a specified age who has violated criminal laws or has engaged in disobedient, indecent or immoral conduct, and is in need of treatment, rehabilitation, or supervision.

District Attorney - An officer of a governmental body with the duty to prosecute those accused of crimes.

Docket - A list of cases on the court's calendar.

Double Jeopardy - Fifth Amendment provision providing that an individual shall not be subject to prosecution for the same offense more than one time.

Due Process Rights - All rights which are of such fundamental importance as to require compliance with due process standards of fairness and justice.

Duress - Refers to the action of one person which compels another to do something he or she would not otherwise do.

Entrapment - In criminal law, refers to the use of trickery by the police to induce the defendant to commit a crime for which he or she has a predisposition to commit.

Exclusionary Rule - A constitutional rule of law providing that evidence procured by illegal police conduct, although otherwise admissible, will be excluded at trial.

Expert Witness - A witness who has special knowledge about a certain subject, upon which he or she will testify, which knowledge is not normally possessed by the average person.

Fact Finder - In a judicial or administrative proceeding, the person, or group of persons, that has the responsibility of determining the acts relevant to decide a controversy.

Fact Finding - A process by which parties present their evidence and make their arguments to a neutral person, who issues a nonbinding report based on the findings, which usually contains a recommendation for settlement.

False Arrest - An unlawful arrest.

False Imprisonment - Detention of an individual without justification.

False Pretense - A statutory offense whereby one obtains the property of another by making a false representation with an intent to defraud.

Federal Courts - The courts of the United States.

Felony - A crime of a graver or more serious nature than those designated as misdemeanors.

Fine - A financial penalty imposed upon a defendant.

Forfeiture - The loss of goods or chattels, as a punishment for some crime or misdemeanor of the party forfeiting, and as a compensation for the offense and injury committed against the one to whom they are forfeited.

Fornication - Unlawful sexual intercourse between two unmarried persons.

Grand Jury - A group of people summoned to court to investigate a crime and hand down an indictment if sufficient evidence is presented to hold the accused for trial.

Guardian - A person who is entrusted with the management of the property and/or person of another who is incapable, due to age or incapacity, to administer their own affairs.

Harmless Error - An error committed by a lower court proceeding which does not substantially violate an appellant's rights to an extent that the lower court proceeding should be modified or overturned.

Hearing - A proceeding during which evidence is taken for the purpose of determining the facts of a dispute and reaching a decision.

Ignorance - Lack of knowledge.

Ignorantia Legis Non Excusat - Latin for "Ignorance of the law is no excuse." Although an individual may not think an act is illegal, the act is still punishable.

Illegal - Against the law.

Imprisonment - The confinement of an individual, usually as punishment for a crime.

Indecent - Offending against modesty; obscene; lewd.

Indictment - A formal written accusation of criminal charges submitted to a grand jury for investigation and indorsement.

Inference - A reasoned deduction based on the given facts.

Information - A written accusation of a crime submitted by the prosecutor to inform the accused and the court of the charges and the facts of the crime.

Jail - Place of confinement where a person in custody of the government awaits trial or serves a sentence after conviction.

Judge - The individual who presides over a court, and whose function it is to determine controversies.

Jurisdiction - The power to hear and determine a case.

Jury - A group of individuals summoned to decide the facts in issue in a lawsuit.

Jury Trial - A trial during which the evidence is presented to a jury so that they can determine the issues of fact, and render a verdict based upon the law as it applies to their findings of fact.

Justification - A just, lawful excuse or reason for an act or failing to act.

Kidnapping - The illegal taking of a person against his or her will.

Lewd - Obscene, lustful, indecent, or lascivious.

Lewdness - Gross indecency so notorious as to tend to corrupt community's morals.

Libel - The false and malicious publication, in printed form, for the purpose of defaming another.

Mann Act - A federal statute prohibiting the transportation of a female across state lines for the purpose of prostitution.

Manslaughter - The unlawful taking of another's life without malice aforethought.

Mens Rea - A guilty mind.

Minor - A person who has not yet reached the age of legal competence, which is designated as 18 in most states.

Miranda Rule - The law requiring a person receive certain warnings concerning the privilege against self-incrimination, prior to custodial interrogation, as set forth in the landmark case of "Miranda v. Arizona."

Misdemeanor - Criminal offenses which are less serious than felonies and carry lesser penalties.

Narcotics - Generic term for any drug which dulls the senses or induces sleep and which commonly becomes addictive after prolonged use.

Not Guilty - The plea of a defendant in a criminal action denying the offense with which he or she is charged.

Objection - The process by which it is asserted that a particular question, or piece of evidence, is improper, and it is requested that the court rule upon the objectionable matter.

Obscene - Objectionable or offensive to accepted standards of decency.

Obscene Material - Material which lacks serious literary, artistic, political or scientific value and, taken as a whole, appeals to the prurient interest and, as such, is not protected by the free speech guarantee of the First Amendment.

Obscenity - The character or quality of being obscene; conduct tending to corrupt the public morals by its indecency or lewdness.

Offense - Any misdemeanor or felony violation of the law for which a penalty is prescribed.

Opinion - The reasoning behind a court's decision.

Original Jurisdiction - The jurisdiction of a court to hear a matter in the first instance.

Overrule - A holding in a particular case is overruled when the same court, or a higher court, in that jurisdiction, makes an opposite ruling in a subsequent case on the identical point of law ruled upon in the prior case.

Parens Patriae - Latin for "parent of his country." Refers to the role of the state as guardian of legally disabled individuals.

Parole - The conditional release from imprisonment whereby the convicted individual serves the remainder of his or her sentence outside of prison as long as he or she is in compliance with the terms and conditions of parole.

Parties - The disputants.

Penal Institution - A place of confinement for convicted criminals.

Perfected Appeal - Refers to the satisfaction of all of the necessary steps for an appellant to proceed with his or her appeal in the appellate court.

Petitioner - One who presents a petition to a court or other body either in order to institute an equity proceeding or to take an appeal from a judgment.

Police Power - The power of the state to restrict private individuals in matters relating to public health, safety, and morality, and to impose such other restrictions as may be necessary to promote the welfare of the general public.

Pornographic - That which is of or pertaining to obscene literature; obscene; licentious.

Precedent - A previously decided case which is recognized as authority for the disposition of future cases.

Presumption of Innocence - In criminal law, refers to the doctrine that an individual is considered innocent of a crime until he or she is proven guilty.

Prima Facie Case - A case which is sufficient on its face, being supported by at least the requisite minimum of evidence, and being free from palpable defects.

Prisoner - One who is confined to a prison or other penal institution for the purpose of awaiting trial for a crime, or serving a sentence after conviction of a crime.

Probable Cause - The standard which must be met in order for there to be a valid search and seizure or arrest.   It includes the showing of facts and circumstances reasonably sufficient and credible to permit the police to obtain a warrant.

Prosecution - The process of pursuing a civil lawsuit or a criminal trial.

Prosecutor - The individual who prepares a criminal case against an individual accused of a crime.

Prurient Interest - The shameful and morbid interest in nudity and sex.

Public Defender - A lawyer hired by the government to represent an indigent person accused of a crime.

Punitive Damages - Compensation in excess of compensatory damages which serves as a form of punishment to the wrongdoer who has exhibited malicious and willful misconduct.

Question of Fact - The fact in dispute which is the province of the trier of fact, i.e. the judge or jury, to decide.

Question of Law - The question of law which is the province of the judge to decide.

Rape - The unlawful sexual intercourse with a female person without her consent.

Rational Basis Test - The constitutional analysis of a law to determine whether it has a reasonable relationship to some legitimate government objective so as to uphold the law.

Reasonable Doubt - The standard of certainty of guilt a juror must have in order to find a defendant guilty of the crime charged.

Respondent - The responding party, also known as the defendant.

Search and Seizure - The search by law enforcement officials of a person or place in order to seize evidence to be used in the investigation and prosecution of a crime.

Search Warrant - A judicial order authorizing and directing law enforcement officials to search a specified location for specific items or individuals.

Sentence - The punishment given a convicted criminal by the court.

Suicide The deliberate termination of one's existence.

Summation - The point in the trial when the attorney for each party sums up the evidence presented in the case, and makes their final argument as to their legal position.

Summons - A mandate requiring the appearance of the defendant in an action under penalty of having judgment entered against him for failure to do so.

Suppression of Evidence - The refusal to produce or permit evidence for use in litigation, such as when there has been an illegal search and seizure of the evidence.

Supreme Court - In most jurisdictions, the Supreme Court is the highest appellate court, including the federal court system.

Taking the Fifth - The term given to an individual's right not to incriminate oneself under the Fifth Amendment.

Testify - The offering of a statement in a judicial proceeding, under oath and subject to the penalty of perjury.

Testimony - The sworn statement make by a witness in a judicial proceeding.

Trial - The judicial procedure whereby disputes are determined based on the presentation of issues of law and fact. Issues of fact are decided by the trier of fact, either the judge or jury, and issues of law are decided by the judge.

Trial Court - The court of original jurisdiction over a particular matter.

Unconstitutional - Refers to a statute which conflicts with the United States Constitution rendering it void.

Undue Influence - The exertion of improper influence upon another for the purpose of destroying that person's free will in carrying out a particular act, such as entering into a contract.

Unreasonable Search and Seizure - A search and seizure which has not met the constitutional requirements under the Fourth and Fourteenth Amendment.

Verdict - The definitive answer given by the jury to the court concerning the matters of fact committed to the jury for their deliberation and determination.

Vice Crimes - Illegal activities which offend the moral standards of the community, such as gambling and prostitution.

Void - Having no legal force or binding effect.

Void for Vagueness - The term given a criminal statute which is so vague that persons of normal intelligence do not comprehend its application, thus rendering it void.

Warrant - An official order directing that a certain act be undertaken, such as an arrest.

Warrantless Arrest - An arrest carried out without a warrant.

BIBLIOGRAPHY

ACLU In Congress. New York, NY: The American Civil Liberties Union, November1995.

ACLU In Congress. New York, NY: The American Civil Liberties Union, December 1995.

ACLU In Congress. New York, NY: The American Civil Liberties Union, January 1996.

Attorney General's Commission on Pornography, Final Report. Washington, DC: U.S. Department of Justice, 1986.

Black's Law Dictionary, Fifth Edition . St. Paul, MN: West Publishing Company, 1979.

Francois, William E.*Mass Media Law and Regulation.* Iowa City, IA: Iowa State University Press, 1990.

Gorman, Carol.*Pornography.* New York, NY: Franklin Watts, Inc., 1988.

Osanka, Franklin M. and Johann, Sara L.*Sourcebook on Pornography.* Lexington, MA: Lexington Books, 1989.

McKinney's Consolidated Laws of New York, Penal Law, Book 89. St. Paul, MN: West Publishing Co., 1989.